the art of
ADORNMENT

First Edition
15 14 13 12 11   5 4 3 2 1

Copyright © 2011 Gibbs Smith, Publisher

Published by
Gibbs Smith
P.O. Box 667
Layton, Utah 84041

1.800.835.4993 orders
www.gibbs-smith.com

Designed by Sheryl Dickert
Printed and bound in China

Gibbs Smith books are printed on either recycled, 100% post-consumer
waste, FSC-certified papers or on paper produced from sustainable PEFC-
certified forest/controlled wood source. Learn more at www.pefc.org.

ISBN: 978-1-4236-2345-8

the art of ADORNMENT

DESIGN · FASHION · ART

GIBBS SMITH

TO ENRICH AND INSPIRE HUMANKIND

DESIGN

ADORNMENT:

that which adorns;

the act of

decorating

Design

is a mix of

CRAFT,

science,

STORYTELLING,

propaganda,

and

PHILOSOPHY.

—ERIK ADIGARD

THE BEST DESIGN TOOL

is a long eraser

WITH A PENCIL AT ONE END.

—MARTY NEUMEIER

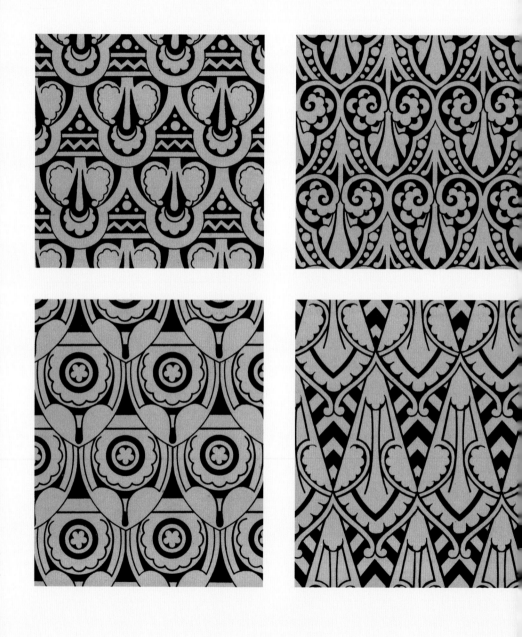

HAVE NO FEAR OF

PERFECTION—

you'll never

reach it.

—SALVADOR DALI

A designer

is a planner with an

aesthetic sense.

—BRUNO MUNARI

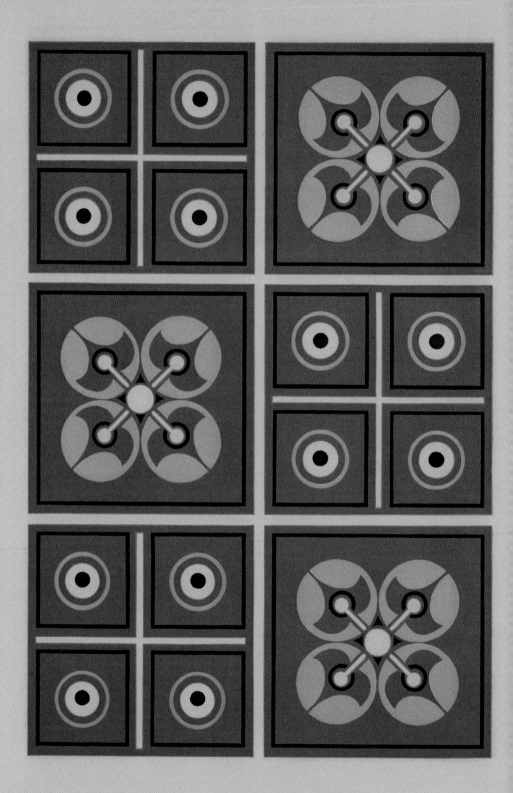

SIMPLICITY

is the ultimate sophistication.

—LEONARDO DA VINCI

GOOD DESIGN

keeps the user happy,

the manufacturer in the black,

AND THE AESTHETE UNOFFENDED.

—RAYMOND LOEWY

Design is not about innovation. Design is about communication. Innovation in design is usually a wonderful byproduct or direct result of a particular need. Design that seeks to foremost be innovative will commonly fall apart under its own stylistic girth.

—JASON SANTA MARIA

Think more,

DESIGN LESS.

—ELLEN LUPTON

DESIGN

is the silent

ambassador of

your brand.

—PAUL RAND

THERE IS NO

design

WITHOUT

discipline.

———————

THERE IS NO

discipline

WITHOUT

intelligence.

—MASSIMO VIGNELLI

Every act of

CREATION

is first an act of

destruction.

—PABLO PICASSO

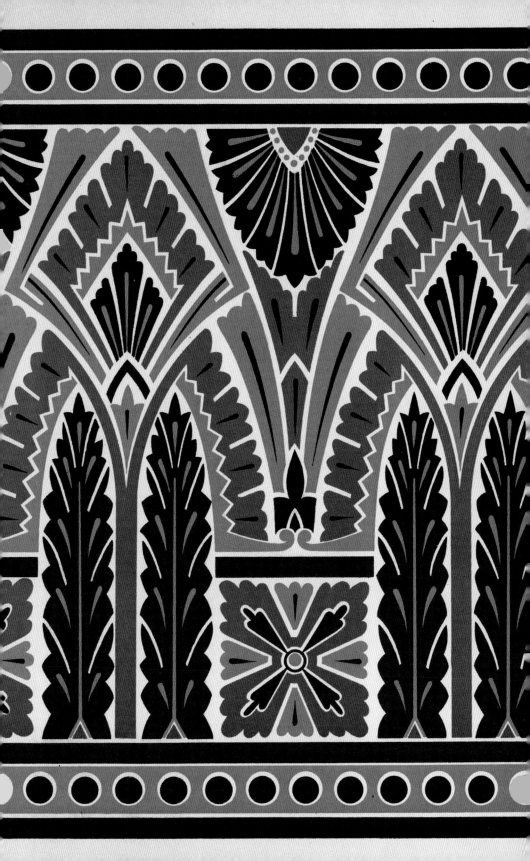

DESIGN IS A PLAN FOR ARRANGING

ELEMENTS IN SUCH A WAY AS BEST TO

ACCOMPLISH A PARTICULAR PURPOSE.

—CHARLES EAMES

FASHION

ADORNMENT:

the action of decorating *Yourself* with something colorful and *interesting*.

FASHION

IS NOT SOMETHING THAT EXISTS IN

DRESSES ONLY. FASHION IS IN THE

SKY, IN THE STREET, FASHION HAS TO

DO WITH IDEAS, THE WAY WE LIVE,

WHAT IS HAPPENING.

—COCO CHANEL

*T*o live content with small means; to seek elegance

rather than luxury, and refinement rather than fash-

ion; to be worthy, not respectable, and wealthy, not,

rich; to listen to stars and birds babes and sages, with

open heart; to study hard; to think quietly, act frankly,

talk gently, await occasions, hurry never; in a word, to

let the spiritual, unbidden, and unconscious, grow up

through the common—*this is my symphony.*

—WILLIAM HENRY CHANNING

As I grew older, I realized that it was much better

to insist on the genuine forms of nature, for

simplicity is the greatest

adornment of art.

—ALBRECHT DURER

Know, first,
who you are;

and then adorn yourself accordingly.

—EPICTETUS

The elegance of

HONESTY

needs no

adornment.

—MERRY BROWNE

One should

either be a

work of art,

or wear a

work of art.

—OSCAR WILDE

ADORNMENT

is never anything except

a reflection of the heart.

—COCO CHANEL

Fashion

is architecture:

it is a matter

of proportion.

—COCO CHANEL

The secret of fashion

is to surprise and never

to disappoint.

—EDWARD G. BULWER-LYTTON

Fashion is about good energy.

IT'S ABOUT FEELINGS.

—ADRIANA LIMA

On peut être plus fin qu'un
autre, mais no plus fin que
tous les autres.

You can be more elegant than

another, but not more elegant

than all the others.

—LA ROCHEFOUCAULD

Beauty of

STYLE

and

HARMONY

and

GRACE

and

GOOD RHYTHM

depend on

SIMPLICITY.

—PLATO

ART

ADORNMENT:

A *decoration* of color or interest that is added to *relieve plainness.*

En art comme en amour,

l'instinct suffit.

WHETHER IT IS ART OR LOVE,

YOUR INSTINCT WILL SUFFICE.

—ANONYMOUS

*E*ach of the arts whose

office is to refine, purify,

adorn, embellish and grace

life is under the patronage

of a muse, no god being

found worthy to preside

over them.

—RALPH WALDO EMERSON

THERE ARE

always

flowers

FOR THOSE WHO

want to

see them.

—HENRI MATISSE

ART IS IDENTICAL WITH

A STATE OF CAPACITY TO

MAKE, INVOLVING A TRUE

COURSE OF REASONING.

—ARISTOTLE

Art COMPLETES WHAT

NATURE CANNOT BRING TO FINISH.

THE ARTIST GIVES US *knowledge*

OF NATURE'S UNREALIZED ENDS.

—ARISTOTLE

Art is a fruit that grows in man,

like a fruit on a plant, or a child

in its mother's womb.

—JEAN ARP

Art is our chief

means of breaking

bread with the dead.

—W.H. AUDEN

Art, when inspired with love,

leads to higher realms.

Love art, and that art will open

for you the inner life.

—MEHER BABA

ART

IS WHO WE ARE.

It facilitates self-realization

in everyone.

—PHILIPPE BENICHOU

La critique est aisée,

CRITICISM IS EASY,

mais l'art est difficile.

ART IS DIFFICULT.

—DESTOUCHES

ALL ART, WHETHER IT PLEASES US

OR NOT, HELPS TO ADD COLOR, EXCITEMENT,

JOY, OR SADNESS AND, MOST OFTEN, A SENSE

OF AWE TO OUR LIFE'S EXPERIENCE.

—HENRY O. DORMANN

Art is frozen zen.

—REGINALD H. BLYTH